Twe

Knitted Fruit

Susie Johns

Search Press

First published in Great Britain 2011

Search Press Limited
Wellwood, North Farm Road,
Tunbridge Wells, Kent TN2 3DR

Reprinted 2011 (twice)

Text copyright © Susie Johns 2011

Photographs by Debbie Patterson at
Search Press Studios

Photographs and design copyright
© Search Press Ltd 2011

ISBN: 978-1-84448-540-6

Suppliers
If you have difficulty in obtaining any of the
materials and equipment mentioned in this book,
then please visit the Search Press website for
details of suppliers: www.searchpress.com

Printed in Malaysia

Dedication
For my mother and grandmothers
who, by teaching me how to knit and
crochet, opened the door to a world
of creative possibilities.

Abbreviations

beg: begin(ning)

dec: decrease (by working two
stitches together)

DK: double knitting

g st: garter stitch (knit every row)

inc: increase (by working into the front and
back of the stitch)

inc1: knit into front and back of same stitch

inc2: knit into front, back and front of stitch

k: knit

k2tog: knit two stitches together

M1: make one stitch

p: purl

psso: pass the slipped stitch over

p2tog: purl two stitches together

rib: ribbing (one stitch knit, one stitch purl)

rem: remain(ing)

rep: repeat(ing)

sl1: slip one stitch on to the right-hand
needle without knitting it

st(s): stitch(es)

st st: stocking stitch (one row knit, one
row purl)

tbl: through back loop

yfwd: yarn forward

yon: yarn over needle

Contents

Introduction

These knitted fruits – some familiar, some quite exotic, depending on where in the world you come from – are fun to make and a great way to use up oddments of yarn.

Like all novelty knitted items, they make great gifts: a single fruit attached to a key ring, perhaps, or a selection arranged in a bowl or basket. They would also be ideal for children (apart from the blackberries, which include small beads) as long as you sew the components together very securely.

Most fruits tend to be round in shape and many of the patterns are designed to be knitted in the round on a set of four double-pointed needles. If this seems rather daunting, start with the simpler designs – the banana and the rhubarb, for example – before moving on to the round fruits. Because most of the projects are small, they are relatively quick to knit, though you should allow extra time for the making up and sewing in of yarn ends.

Where round shapes are knitted on two needles, you will need to stitch edges together neatly and it is worth learning how to graft a seam as this produces the tidiest result.

Fruit Basket
With needles, yarn and basic knitting stitches, you can create a cornucopia of colourful fruits.

Materials and techniques

Tensions (or gauges) for the projects are not given: just aim for a firm, close-knit fabric that will hold its shape and not allow the stuffing to poke through. You will see that the needle sizes given in the patterns are smaller than you might expect. But you may decide to use a larger or smaller needle than the one stated in the pattern, depending on whether you are a 'tight' or a 'loose' knitter, to produce the desired effect.

The projects are mostly made from double knitting (DK) yarn, though some of the smaller items use four-ply. As a general rule, I prefer to use natural fibres in my knitting projects, particularly pure wool, cashmere, cotton and silk – but in some cases I have had to use acrylic yarns and various blends in order to source suitable fruity colours.

The amounts given in the patterns assume that you are buying yarn and so are stated in balls – but before you go shopping for yarns, experiment with any oddments you may already have. Search your yarn stash for shades of yellow, green, orange, red, plum, purple and peach, as well as some white and brown and you should have enough to make a start. If you need to buy only a small amount of a certain colour, tapestry yarns are a good choice as they are sold in small skeins and are available in a wider choice of colours than most knitting yarns.

Knitting note
Where the pattern states 'inc1', knit into the front and back of the stitch, thereby creating one extra stitch. Where the pattern states 'inc2', knit into the front, the back and the front again, thereby creating two extra stitches.

Knitting note
When working with four double-pointed needles, if you find you are having trouble starting the patterns with only a few stitches, try knitting the first row on only two needles then distribute the stitches to the four needles and continue working.

Pear

Materials:
1 ball DK cotton yarn – pale green

Polyester fibrefill

Tapestry needle

Needles:
Set of four 3.25mm (UK 10; US 3) double-pointed knitting needles

Instructions:

Pear (make 1)
With size 3.25mm (UK 10; US 3) double-pointed knitting needles and pale green yarn, cast on 12 sts and divide between three needles.

Round 1: k.

Round 2: inc1 in each st [24 sts].

Round 3: k.

Round 4: (inc1, k1) 12 times [36 sts].

Rounds 5–7: k.

Round 8: (inc1, k2) 12 times [48 sts].

Rounds 9–20: k.

Round 21: (k2tog, k2) 12 times [36 sts].

Rounds 22–27: k.

Round 28: (k2tog, k1) 12 times [24 sts].

Rounds 29–33: k.

Round 34: (k2tog) 12 times [12 sts].

Rounds 35–36: k.

Round 37: (k2tog) 6 times.

Cut yarn and thread through rem 6 sts; fasten off.

Stalk (make 1)
With two 3.25mm double-pointed needles and brown yarn, cast on 3 sts.

Row 1: k3; do not turn but slide sts to other end of needle.

Rep row 1 until cord measures 4cm (1¾in); cut yarn, leaving a tail. Fasten off.

Making up
Stuff the pear with polyester fibrefill, then pull the yarn to close the stitches on the last row, inserting one end of the stalk as you do so. Secure the stalk with one or two discreet stitches, then thread the tail of the yarn in and out of the last two stitches to create a knobbly end to the stalk. With spare brown yarn, embroider a small star on the base of the pear (see detail).

The finished pear measures 12cm (4in) high, excluding the stalk.

Nice Pear

The same yarn in pale yellow makes the perfect partner for the green pear.

Banana

Materials:

2 balls DK yarn – 1 yellow and 1 ivory

Polyester fibrefill

18cm (7in) zip – yellow

Sewing thread – yellow

Tapestry needle

Sewing needle

Needles:

1 pair 3.25mm (UK 10; US 3) knitting needles

1 set of four 2.75mm (UK 12; US 2) double-pointed knitting needles

Instructions:

Banana skin (make 1)

With size 3.25mm (UK 10; US 3) needles, cast on 12 sts in yellow yarn.

Row 1 (RS): (k2, p1) 4 times.

Row 2: (k1, p2) 4times.

Rows 3–6: Rep rows 1 and 2 twice more.

Row 7: (inc 1, inc 1, p1) 4 times [20 sts].

Row 8: (k1, p4) 4 times.

Row 9: *(k1, inc 1) twice, p1, rep from * 3 times more [28 sts].

Row 10: (k1, p6) 4 times.

Row 11: (k6, p1) 4 times.

Rows 12–60: Rep rows 10 and 11, ending with row 10 to start the next knit row.

Row 61: (sl1, k1, psso, k2, k2tog, p1) 4 times [20 sts].

Row 62: (k1, p4) 4 times.

Row 63: (sl1, k1, psso, k2tog, p1) 4 times [12 sts].

Row 64: p2tog 6 times [6 sts].

Row 65: k.

Row 66: p.

Rows 67–70: Rep rows 65 and 66 twice more.

Cast off knitwise; cut yarn, leaving a long tail for sewing up.

Banana (make 1)

With 2.75mm (UK 12; US 2) double-pointed knitting needles and ivory yarn, cast on 12 sts and divide between three needles.

Rounds 1 and 2: k.

Round 3: (k1, inc 1) 6 times [18 sts].

Round 4: k.

Round 5: (k2, inc 1) 6 times [24 sts].

Round 6: k.

Round 7: (k7, inc 1) 3 times [27 sts].

Rounds 8–64: k; or until work measures 18cm (7in) from beg.

Round 65: (k7, k2tog) 3 times [24 sts].

Round 66: k.

Round 67: (k2, k2tog) 6 times [18 sts].

Round 68: k.

Round 69: (k1, k2tog) 6 times [12 sts].

Round 70: k.

Break yarn and thread through rem sts.

Making up

Insert an 18cm (7in) zip in the banana skin. Stuff the banana and close the end by threading yarn through all the stitches. Pull up tightly and fasten off. The finished banana measures approximately 21cm (8¼in) long and 5cm (2in) in diameter.

Unzip a Banana

Instead of inserting a zip, graft the two long edges of the banana skin together and pull up the yarn tightly to shorten the seam, thereby causing the banana to bend. Before completing the seam, stuff the banana skin.

11

Strawberry

Materials:

1 ball DK wool or acrylic yarn – red

Small amount of DK wool or acrylic yarn – green

Polyester fibrefill

Tapestry needle

Needles:

1 pair 3.25mm (UK 10; US 3) knitting needles

1 pair 3.00mm (UK 11; US 2) knitting needles

Instructions:

Strawberry

With size 3.25mm (UK 10; US 3) needles and red yarn, cast on 6 sts.

Row 1: (inc1, k1) 3 times [9sts].
Row 2: p.
Row 3: (inc1, k2) 3 times [12 sts].
Row 4: p.
Row 5: (inc1, k3) 3 times [15 sts].
Row 6: p.
Row 7: (inc1, k4) 3 times [18 sts].
Row 8: p.
Row 9: (inc1, k2) 6 times [24 sts].
Row 10: p.
Row 11: (inc1, k3) 6 times [30 sts].
Row 12: p.
Row 13: k.
Row 14: p.
Row 15: (k2tog, k3) 6 times [24 sts].
Row 16: (k2tog) 12 times [12 sts].
Row 17: (k2tog) 6 times [6 sts].
Row 18: (k2tog) 3 times [3 sts].
Cast off.

Calyx and stalk

*With 3.00mm (UK 11; US 2) needles and green yarn, cast on 1 st.

Row 1: (RS) k.
Row 2: inc2 [3 sts].
Row 3: k1, p1, k1.
Row 4: k.
Row 5: k1, p1, k1.
Row 6: k1, inc2 in next st, k1 [5 sts].
Row 7: k1, p3, k1.
Row 8: k.
Row 9: k1, p3, k1; cut yarn and transfer sts to a stitch holder or spare needle.*

Rep from * to * 3 times more.

With right side of work facing, k across all sts on spare needle [20 sts].

Row 10: (p2tog) 10 times [10 sts].

Cut yarn and thread through the first 8 sts, leaving 2 sts on needle for stalk.

Row 11: k2; do not turn but slide sts to other end of needle.

Rows 12–15: Rep row 11 4 times more; then fasten off.

Making up

Graft the edges of the strawberry together, stuffing it with polyester fibrefill as you go. On the calyx, turn under the edges on each point, using the yarn ends to secure, then stitch it to the top of the strawberry.

Strawberries and Dreams

Make a whole punnetful of strawberries, with or without stalks, as a celebration of summer.

Lemon Slice

Materials:

1 ball DK acrylic yarn – lemon yellow

Small amount DK acrylic yarn – white

Craft foam, 2mm (¹⁄₁₆in) thick

Tapestry needle and thread

Needles:

Set of five double-pointed 3.00mm
(UK 11; US 2) knitting needles

Instructions:

Lemon slice

With set of five size 3.00mm (UK 11; US 2)
double-pointed needles and white yarn,
cast on 6 sts and distribute equally between
three needles.

Round 1: k all sts; cut white yarn and continue
in yellow.

Round 2: inc1 in each st [12 sts].

Round 3: (inc1, k1) 6 times [18 sts].

Round 4: (inc1, k2) 6 times [24 sts].

Round 5: (inc1, k3) 6 times [30 sts].

Round 6: (inc1, k4) 6 times [36 sts].

Round 7: (inc1, k5) 6 times [42 sts].

Round 8: (inc1, k6) 6 times [48 sts].

Join in white yarn (but do not cut yellow).

Round 9: with white yarn, (inc1, k7) 6 times
[54 sts].

With yellow yarn, knit 3 rounds.

Round 13: with white yarn, (k2tog, k7) 6
times [48 sts].

Cut white yarn and continue in yellow.

Round 14: (k2tog, k6) 6 times [42 sts].

Round 15: (k2tog, k5) 6 times [36 sts].

Round 16: (k2tog, k4) 6 times [30 sts].

Round 17: (k2tog, k3) 6 times [24 sts].

Round 18: (k2tog, k2) 6 times [18 sts].

Round 19: (k2tog, k1) 6 times [12 sts].

Round 20: (k2tog) 6 times.

Cut yarn, leaving a tail, and thread
through rem 6 sts.

Making up

Cut a 6cm (2³⁄₈in) disc of 2mm (¹⁄₁₆in) craft
foam and insert it into the knitted shape.
Thread a tapestry needle with white yarn and
embroider lines radiating from the centre of
the lemon slice. Embroider pips in detached
chain stitch. The finished lemon slice measures
approximately 6cm (2³⁄₈in) in diameter.

Ice and a Slice

A slice of lemon is just the thing to add to a drink – a knitted drink, of course! If you prefer a lime slice, use green yarn and work as for lemon until round 6 has been completed. Change to white yarn and work round 7. Knit 3 rounds in green, then work round 13 in white and rounds 14 onwards in green. The finished lime slice is approximately 5.5cm (2¼in) in diameter.

Lemon

Materials:

1 balls DK wool yarn – lemon yellow

Polyester fibrefill

Tapestry needle

Needles:

Set of four 3.25mm (UK 10; US 3) double-
pointed knitting needles

Instructions:

Lemon

With set of four size 3.25mm (UK 10; US 3)
double-pointed needles and lemon yellow yarn,
cast on 6 sts and distribute between
three needles.

Round 1: k.

Round 2: inc 1 in each st [12 sts].

Round 3: (k1, inc 1) 6 times [18 sts].

Round 4: (k2, inc 1) 6 times [24 sts].

Round 5: (k3, inc 1) 6 times [30 sts].

Round 6: k.

Round 7: (k4, inc 1) 6 times [36 sts].

Knit 11 rounds.

Round 19: (k4, k2tog) 6 times [30 sts].

Round 20: k

Round 21: (k3, k2tog) 6 times [24 sts].

Round 22: (k2, k2tog) 6 times [18 sts].

Round 23: (k1, k2tog) 6 times [12 sts].

Round 24: k2tog six times [6 sts].

Knit 3 rounds.

Break yarn and thread through rem sts.

Making up

Pull up the stitches on the last row. Insert the
stuffing through the small hole at the cast-
on end, then thread the yarn through all the
stitches. Pull up tightly to close the shape,
then fasten off. The finished lemon measures
approximately 8.5cm (3⅜in) long and 6cm
(2⅜in) in diameter.

Knitting note

If you find it easier, you can begin to add
stuffing after round 22.

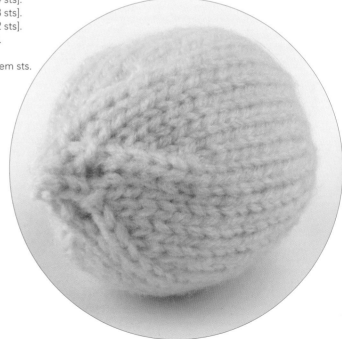

Lemon and Lime

Make a lime by following the pattern using the appropriate shade of green yarn and 3.00mm (UK 11; US 2) needles so it ends up slightly smaller – about 8cm (3¼in) long and 5.5cm (2¼in) in diameter.

Orange

Materials:

1 ball DK wool or acrylic yarn – orange

Small amount DK wool or acrylic yarn – green

Polyester fibrefill

Tapestry needle

Needles:

1 pair 3.25mm (UK 10; US 3) knitting needles

Instructions:

Orange

With 3.25mm (UK 10; US 3) needles and orange yarn, cast on 12 sts.
Row 1 (RS): k.
Row 2: p.
Row 3: inc1 in each st to end [24 sts].
Row 4: p.
Row 5: (inc1, k1) 12 times [36 sts].
Row 6: p.
Row 7: k1 (inc1, k2) 11 times, inc1, k1 [48 sts].
Beg with a p row, work 17 rows in st st (1 row purl, 1 row knit).
Row 25: k1, k2tog, *k2, k2tog; rep from * to last st, k1 [36 sts].
Row 26: p.
Row 27: (k1, k2tog) 12 times [24 sts].
Row 28: (p2tog) 12 times [12 sts].
Row 29: (k2tog) 6 times [6 sts].
Cut yarn, leaving a tail, and thread through rem sts.

Making up

Pull up the tail of yarn to gather the stitches on the final row, then graft the edges of the orange together, stuffing it as you go. Thread a tapestry needle with green yarn and embroider a 'star' of straight stitches at the top (see detail). The finished orange measures approximately 22cm (8½in) in circumference.

Oranges from China

For a satsuma, follow the pattern for the orange from rows 1–5, work 13 rows in stocking stitch, then resume pattern from row 27 to end. For a clementine or other smaller citrus fruit, use the same yarn but smaller needles. For a kumquat, follow the instructions for the cherry on page 26 but use 3.25mm (UK 10; US 3) needles and DK yarn.

Pineapple

Materials:

1 ball wool/cotton blend yarn – yellow

1 ball DK bamboo blend yarn – green

Polyester fibrefill

Tapestry needle and thread

Needles:

1 pair 3.25mm (UK 10; US 3) knitting needles

1 pair 2.75mm (UK 12; US 2) knitting needles

Instructions:

Pineapple (make one)

With 3.25mm (UK 10; US 3) needles and yellow DK yarn, cast on 6 sts.

Row 1: k.

Row 2: (k1, inc1) 3 times [9 sts].

Row 3: k.

Row 4: k1, (inc2 in next st, k1) 4 times [17 sts].

Row 5: k.

Row 6: k2, (inc2 in next st, k3) 3 times, inc2 in next st, k2 [25 sts].

Row 7: k.

Row 8: k3, (inc2 in next st, k5) 3 times, inc2 in next st, k3 [33 sts].

Row 9: k.

Row 10: k4, (inc2 in next st, k7) 3 times, inc2 in next st, k4 [41 sts].

Row 11: k5, (p1, k9) 3 times, p1, k5.

Row 12: k4, (inc1, p1, inc1, k7) 3 times, inc1, p1, inc1, k4 [49 sts].

Row 13: k6, (p1, k11) 3 times, p1, k6.

Row 14: k5, (inc1, p1, inc1, k9) 3 times, inc1, p1, inc1, k5 [57 sts].

Work 4-row pattern repeat 8 times.

> **Pattern repeat**
>
> Rows 1 and 3: k.
>
> Row 2: K1, *p3tog but do not transfer to right-hand needle, yon and p3tog again, k1, rep from * to end.
>
> Row 4: k1, p1, k1, *p3tog but do not transfer to right-hand needle, yon and p3tog again, k1, rep from * to last 2 sts, p1, k1 [57 sts].

Row 47: k1, (p3tog, k1) 14 times [25 sts].

Row 48: k.

Row 49: k2, (k2tog, k4) 4 times, k2tog, k3 [21 sts].

Row 50: k.

Row 51: k2, (k2tog, k3) 4 times, k2tog, k2 [17 sts].

Row 52: k.

Row 53: k1, (k2tog, k2) 4 times [13 sts].

Row 54: k.

Row 55: k1, (k2tog, k1) 4 times.

Cut yarn, leaving a long tail, and thread through rem 9 sts.

Long leaf (make seven)

With 2.75mm (UK 12; US 2) needles and green DK, cast on 7 sts.

Row 1: k2tog, yfwd, k1, p1, k1, yfwd, k2tog.

Row 2: k1, (p2, k1) twice.

Rep rows 1 and 2 7 times more.

Row 17: k2tog, k1, p1, k1, k2tog [5 sts].

Row 18: k1, (p1, k1) twice.

Row 19: k2, p1, k2.

Rep rows 18 and 19 twice more then row 18 once more.

Row 25: k2tog, p1, k2tog [3 sts].

Row 26: k3.

Row 27: k1, p1, k1.

Row 28: k3.

Row 29: sl1, k2tog, psso; fasten off.

Short leaf (make five)

With 2.75mm (UK 12; US 2) needles and green DK, cast on 7 sts.
Row 1: k2tog, yfwd, k1, p1, k1, yfwd, k2tog.
Row 2: k1, (p2, k1) twice.
Rep rows 1 and 2 4 times more.
Continue as for long leaf from row 17 to end.

Making up

Join the edges of the pineapple with a neat backstitch seam, turning it right sides out and stuffing it firmly with polyester fibrefill before completing and closing the seam. Stitch the bases of leaves together to form a bundle (see detail opposite), with the long leaves in the centre and the short leaves all around. Insert the base of the bundle into the top of the pineapple and stitch it firmly in place.

The finished pineapple measures approximately 12cm (4¾in) high and 25cm (10in) in circumference.

Fresh off the Boat

Real pineapples are delicious, and very good for you as they are full of vitamin C. This knitted one is simply very high in fibre!

Watermelon Slice

Materials:

2 balls DK wool or wool blend yarn – 1 red,
1 white

1 ball wool or wool blend aran weight yarn –
dark green

Small amount of DK wool yarn or tapestry yarn
– black

Polyester fibrefill

Tapestry needle

Needles:

Set of four 3.25mm (UK 10; US 3) double-
pointed knitting needles

1 pair 3.25mm (UK 10; US 3) knitting needles

Instructions:

Watermelon flesh (make 1)

With set of four 3.25mm (UK 10; US 3)
double-pointed needles and red yarn, cast on
6 sts and distribute between three needles.
Round 1: inc1 in each st to end [12 sts].
Round 2: (k1, inc1) 6 times [18 sts].
Round 3: (k2, inc1) 6 times [24 sts].
Round 4: (k3, inc1) 6 times [30 sts].
Round 5: (k4, inc1) 6 times [36 sts].
Round 6: (k5, inc1) 6 times [42 sts].
Round 7: (k6, inc1) 6 times [48 sts].
Round 8: (k7, inc1) 6 times [54 sts].
Round 9: (k8, inc1) 6 times [60 sts].
Round 10: (k9, inc1) 6 times [66 sts].
Round 11: k5, (inc1, k10) 5 times, k5 [71 sts].
Round 12: k6, (inc1, k11) 5 times, k5 [76 sts].
Round 13: k7, (inc1, k12) 5 times, k5 [81 sts].
Round 14: k8, (inc1, k13) 5 times, k5 [86 sts].
Round 15: k9, (inc1, k14) 5 times, k5 [91 sts].
Round 16: k10, (inc1, k15) 5 times, k5 [96 sts].
Round 17: k11, (inc1, k16) 5 times, k5 [101 sts].
Round 18: k12, (inc1, k17) 5 times, k5 [106 sts].
Round 19: k13, (inc1, k18) 5 times, k5 [111 sts].
Round 20: k14, (inc1, k19) 5 times, k5 [116 sts].
Round 21: k15, (inc1, k20) 5 times, k5 [121 sts];
cut red yarn and join in white.
Round 22: k16, (inc1, k21) 5 times, k5 [126 sts].
Round 23: k.
Cast off.

Rind (make 1)

With 3.25mm (UK 10; US 3) needles and dark
green yarn, cast on 1 st.
Row 1: inc2 in next st [3 sts].
Row 2: k1, p1, k1.
Row 3: k1, inc2 in next st, k1 [5 sts].
Row 4: k1, p3, k1.
Row 5: k1, (inc1, k1) twice [7 sts].
Row 6: k1, p5, k1.
Row 7: k1, inc1, k3, inc 1, k1 [9 sts].
Row 8: k1, p7, k1.
Row 9: k.
Rep rows 8 and 9 until rind almost fits around
half circumference of watermelon flesh piece.
Next row: k1, k2tog, k3, k2tog, k1 [7 sts].
Next row: k1, p5, k1.
Next row: k1, (k2tog, k1) twice [5 sts].
Next row: k1, p3, k1.
Next row: k1, sl1, k2tog, psso, k1 [3 sts].
Next row: p3tog. Fasten off.

Making up
Fold the main piece in half with the purl side facing outwards. Backstitch along the fold, then stitch the rind to the flesh, leaving a small gap. Stuff the watermelon fairly firmly before stitching the gap closed. Embroider detached chain stitches on to the surface of the watermelon to depict seeds. The finished watermelon slice measures approximately 17cm (6¾in) long and 9cm (3½in) wide.

Knitting note
Remember, to increase 1 (inc1), knit into the front and the back of the same stitch. To increase 2 (inc2), knit into front, back and front of same stitch.

Sweet Watermelon
Few things are more refreshing than a delicious slice of watermelon; and they are nearly as good to look at as they are to eat!

Bunch of Grapes

Materials:

1 ball four-ply wool or wool blend yarn – purple
Small amount of DK wool yarn – brown
Polyester fibrefill
Tapestry needle

Needles:

1 pair 2.25mm (UK 13; US 1) knitting needles
Two 3.00mm (UK 11; US 2) double-pointed
knitting needles

Instructions:

Large grape (make 7)

With 2.25mm (UK 13; US 1) needles and purple
yarn, cast on 6 sts.
Row 1 and all odd-numbered (WS) rows until
row 19: p.
Row 2: inc1 in each st [12 sts].
Row 4: (k1, inc1) 6 times [18 sts].
Row 6: (k2, inc1) 6 times [24 sts].
Beg with a p row, work 7 rows in st st (1 row p,
1 row k).
Row 14: (k2, k2tog) 6 times [18 sts].
Row 16: (k1, k2tog) 6 times [12 sts].
Row 18: (k2tog) 6 times [6 sts].
Row 19: (p2tog) 3 times; cut yarn, leaving a tail,
and thread through rem 3 sts.

Small grape (make 9)

With 2.25mm (UK 13; US 1) needles and purple
yarn, cast on 6 sts.
Row 1 and all odd-numbered (WS) rows
until row 13: p.
Row 2: inc1 in each st [12 sts].
Row 4: (k1, inc1) 6 times [18 sts].
Beg with a p row, work 5 rows st st.
Row 10: (k1, k2tog) 6 times [12 sts].
Row 12: (k2tog) 6 times [6 sts].
Row 13: (p2tog) 3 times; cut yarn, leaving a tail,
and thread through rem 3 sts.

Stalk (make 1)

With 3.00mm (UK 11; US 2) double-pointed
needles and brown yarn, cast on 4 sts.
Row 1: k4; do not turn but slide sts to other end
of needle.

Rep row 1 12 times more, then turn and cast on
3 sts [7 sts].
Row 14: k to end, turn and cast on 3 sts [10 sts].
Row 15: k.
Cast off.

Making up

Graft the edges of each grape together and
stuff firmly. Pull up the tail of yarn to pull the
stitches on the last row together. Make a cluster
of three small grapes by passing a tail of yarn
through one end of each, then pulling it up
tightly before fastening it off. Thread a tapestry
needle with two strands of purple four-ply yarn,
then join the end of the yarn to one end of one
small grape and pass the needle up through
the centre of the cluster of three grapes.

Make another cluster in the same way, this
time of five small grapes, and pass the needle
up through the centre. Make a cluster of four
large grapes and pass the needle up through
the centre; then a cluster of three large grapes;
fasten the yarn firmly to the centre of this
cluster. Finally, pass the needle through the end
of the stalk and stitch it firmly in place. On the
top (cast-off) edge of the stalk, fold over the
cast-off row and oversew using matching yarn.

The finished bunch measures approximately
13cm (5⅛in), excluding the stalk.

The Grapes of Fluff

*Delicious grapes are even better if you
can convince someone to peel them
and feed them to you.*

Cherries

Materials:
1 ball four-ply wool yarn – red
Small amounts of four-ply wool yarn – green
Stitch holder
Tapestry needle
Polyester fibrefill

Needles:
1 pair of 2.25mm (UK 13; US 1) knitting needles
Two 2.25mm (UK 13; US 1) double-pointed
   knitting needles

Instructions:

Cherry (make 2)
With size 2.25mm (UK 13; US 1) double-pointed needles and red yarn, cast on 3 sts.
Row 1 and all odd-numbered (WS) rows until row 19: p to end.
Row 2: inc1 in each st [6 sts].
Row 4: inc1 in each st [12 sts].
Row 6: (k1, inc1) 6 times [18 sts].
Row 8: (k2, inc1) 6 times [24 sts].
Rows 9 –13: Beg with a purl row, work in st st (1 row p, 1 row k).
Row 14: (k2, k2tog) 6 times [18 sts].
Row 16: (k1, k2tog) 6 times [12 sts].
Row 18: (k2tog) 6 times [6 sts].
Row 19: (p2tog) 3 times.
Break yarn, leaving a tail, and thread through rem 3 sts.

Stalk
**With 2.25mm (UK 13; US 1) double-pointed needles and green yarn, cast on 2 sts.
Row 1: k2; do not turn but slide sts to other end of needle.
Rows 2–18: Rep row 1 17 times more; do not fasten off**.
Leave sts on a stitch holder or spare needle and make a second stalk by repeating instructions from ** to **.
Slip sts on holder back on to needle [4 sts], knit across all sts, then cast off and cut yarn, leaving a tail.

Making up
On each cherry, pull up the tail of yarn to close the stitches on the last row, then thread the yarn on to a tapestry needle. Stitch the side seam using a grafting technique, adding stuffing before reaching the end of the seam. Insert the end of the stalk into the gap on the cast-on edge, then run the end of the yarn through all the stitches on the cast-on edge and pull up to close. Using the tail of yarn at the top of the stalk, oversew the cast-off row and pull up firmly before fastening off.
   The finished cherry measures approximately 2.5cm (1in) in diameter.

Cheery Cherry

Cherries can be made into pies, soup or even wine; but these knitted versions are best kept as decorations! You could attach a brooch back to the stalk and wear the cherry as a delightful accessory.

Peach

Materials:

2 balls DK bamboo blend viscose yarn – 1 peach, 1 pale peach

Small amounts of DK wool or wool blend yarn – brown and leaf green

Polyester fibrefill

Tapestry needle

Needles:

1 pair 3.25mm (UK 10; US 3) knitting needles

Two 2.75mm (UK 12; US 2) double-pointed knitting needles

Instructions:

Peach

With 3.25mm (UK 10; US 3) needles and peach yarn, cast on 6sts.
Row 1 and every odd-numbered (RS) row: p.
Row 2: inc1 in each st [12 sts].
Row 4: (k1, inc1) 6 times [18 sts].
Row 6: k1, inc1, (k2, inc1) 5 times, k1 [24 sts].
Row 8: k2, inc1, (k3, inc1) 5 times, k1 [30 sts].
Rows 9– 15: Beg with a purl row, work in st st for 7 rows. Cut yarn and join in pale peach yarn.
Rows 16–23: Work in st st for a further 8 rows.
Row 24: (k3, k2tog) 6 times [24 sts].
Row 26: (k2, k2tog) 6 times [18 sts].
Row 28: (k1, k2tog) 6 times [12 sts].
Row 30: (k2tog tbl) 6 times [6 sts].
Row 32: (k2tog tbl) 3 times. Cut yarn and thread through rem 3 sts.

Leaf

With two 2.75mm (UK 12; US 2) double-pointed needles and green yarn, cast on 3 sts.
Row 1: k.
Row 2 and every even-numbered row: p to end.
Row 3: (inc1 in next st) twice, k1 [5 sts].
Row 5: k1, inc1 in each of next 2 sts, k2 [7 sts].
Row 7: k2, inc1 in each of next 2 sts, k3 [9 sts].
Row 9: k2, sl1, k1, psso, k2tog, k3 [7 sts].
Row 11: k1, sl1, k1, psso, k2tog, k2 [5 sts].
Row 13: sl1, k1, psso, k2tog, k1 [3 sts].

Row 14: push sts to other end of needle, k3.
Rows 15–16: Rep row 14.
Cast off.

Stalk

With two 2.75mm (UK 12; US 2) double-pointed needles and brown yarn, cast on 2 sts.
Row 1: k2; do not turn but slide sts to other end of needle.
Rows 2–8: Rep row 1.
Row 9: Rep row 1, then turn.
Row 10: inc1 in each st (4 sts).
Cast off.

Making up

Stitch the seam using a grafting technique. Stuff fairly firmly. Run the yarn through each stitch on the cast-off edge and pull up tightly, trapping the lower end of the stem in the centre of the hole as you do so. Then take the needle down through the centre of the peach, pulling slightly to create a dimple in the top. Stitch the leaf to the base of the stem.

The finished peach is approximately 7cm (2¾in) tall, excluding the stalk, and 6cm (2⅜in) in diameter.

Just Peachy

Peaches have been cultivated since the tenth century in their native China.

Rhubarb

Materials:

1 ball DK cotton yarn – ivory

2 balls DK wool or wool blend yarn – 1 claret
and 1 apple green

Polyester fibrefill

30cm (12in) length of 25mm (1in) diameter
polyurethane tubing

Stitch holder

Tapestry needle

Needles:

1 pair 3.00mm (UK 11; US 2) knitting needles

Two 3.00mm (UK 11; US 2) double-pointed
knitting needles

Instructions:

Rhubarb stalk

With 3.00mm (UK 11; US 2) needles and ivory
yarn, cast on 1 st.
Row 1: inc2 [3 sts].
Row 2: p3.
Row 3 (RS): inc1, k1, inc1 [5 sts].
Rows 4–14: Beg with a p row, work in st st
(1 row purl, 1 row knit). Cut yarn.
With RS facing, join claret DK yarn to first st and
cast on 8 sts.
Row 15: k [13 sts].
Row 16: cast on 8 sts, p to end [21 sts].
Row 17 (WS): p1, (k1, p1) 10 times.
Row 18: k1, (p1, k1) 10 times.
Rep rows 17 and 18 until work measures 32cm
(12½in), ending with a WS row. Cast off.

Leaf

With 3.00mm (UK 11; US 2) needles and apple
green yarn, cast on 3 sts.
Row 1 (WS): p.
Row 2: k1, (yfwd, k1) twice [5 sts].
Row 3: k2, p1, k2.
Row 4: k2, yfwd, k1, yfwd, k2 [7 sts].
Row 5: k3, p1, k3.
Row 6: k3, yfwd, k1, yfwd, k3 [9 sts].
Row 7: k4, p1, k4.
Row 8: k4, yfwd, k1, yfwd, k4 [11 sts].
Row 9: k5, p1, k5.
Row 10: (k2, yfwd, k1, yfwd) 3 times, k2 [17 sts].

Row 11: k3, (p1, k4) twice, p1, k3.
Row 12: k3, yfwd, k1, yfwd, k4, yfwd, k1, yfwd,
k4, yfwd, k1, yfwd, k3 [23 sts].
Row 13: k4, (p1, k6) twice, p1, k4.
Row 14: k4, yfwd, k1, yfwd, k6, yfwd, k1, yfwd,
k6, yfwd, k1, yfwd, k4 [29 sts].
Row 15: k5, (p1, k8) twice, p1, k5.
Row 16: k5, yfwd, k1, yfwd, k8, yfwd, k1, yfwd,
k8, yfwd, k1, yfwd, k5 [35 sts].
Row 17: k6, (p1, k10) twice, p1, k6.
Row 18: k6, yfwd, k1, yfwd, k6, turn and leave
rem sts on a holder.
Row 19: **k7, p1, k7.
Row 20: k7, yfwd, k1, yfwd, k7 [17 sts].
Row 21: k8, p1, k8.
Row 22: k8, yfwd, k1, yfwd, k8 [19 sts].
Row 23: k9, p1, k9.
Row 24: k.
Row 25: as row 23.
Row 26 and each even-numbered (RS) row: sl1,
k1, psso, k to last 2 sts, k2tog.
Row 27: k8, p1, k8.
Row 29: k7, p1, k7.
Row 31: k6, p1, k6.
Row 33: k5, p1, k5.
Row 35: k4, p1, k4.** Cast off.
Leave centre 9 sts on a holder and rejoin yarn
to rem sts.
Next row: k6, yfwd, k1, yfwd, k6.
Then work rows 19–35 (from ** to **); cast off.
Rejoin yarn to sts on holder with RS facing.
Next row: k4, yfwd, k1, yfwd, k4 [11 sts].
Next row: k5, p1, k5.

Next row: k5, yfwd, k1, yfwd, k5 [13 sts].
Next row: k6, p1, k6.
Next row: k6, yfwd, k1, yfwd, k6.
Then work rows 19–35 (from ** to **); cast off.

Leaf veins

Central vein (make 1)
With 3.00mm (UK 11; US 2) double-pointed needles and claret yarn, cast on 3 sts.
Row 1: k3; do not turn but slide sts to other end of needle.
Rows 2–20: Rep row 1.
Cast off.

Side veins (make 2)
With 3.00mm (UK 11; US 2) double-pointed needles and claret yarn, cast on 2 sts.
Row 1: k3; do not turn but slide sts to other end of needle.
Rows 2–16: Rep row 1.
Cast off.

Making up
Stitch the long edges of the stalk together. Cut the polyurethane tubing in half lengthways and insert one half into the stalk. With the seam running down the centre front of the rhubarb stalk, fold up the ivory-coloured flap at the root end and stitch it in place. Close the top end of the stalk and stitch the ends of the leaf veins to the centre top, then stitch the leaf veins to the centre of each leaf.

The finished rhubarb stalk measures approximately 30cm (12in) long, excluding the leaves, and 3cm (1¼in) wide.

Knitting Note
To increase 2 (inc2), knit into the front, the back and then the front of the stitch.

Rhubarb, Rhubarb, Rhubarb...

If you wish, you can omit the leaves and make a rhubarb stalk that is ready to chop up and bake in a pie.

Sharon Fruit

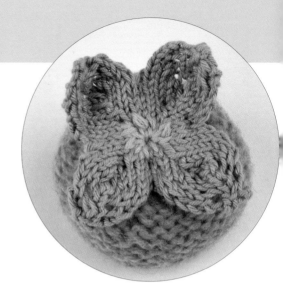

Materials:

1 ball DK wool yarn – light orange

1 ball four-ply cotton yarn – sage green

Small amount of four-ply cotton yarn – grey-green

Polyester fibrefill

Tapestry needle

Needles:

1 pair 3.00mm (UK 11; US 2) knitting needles

1 pair 2.25mm (UK 13; US 1) knitting needles

Instructions:

Sharon fruit

With 3.00mm (UK 11; US 2) needles and light orange yarn, cast on 10 sts.
Row 1 and every odd-numbered (RS) row: p to end.
Row 2: inc1 in each st [20 sts].
Row 4: (inc1, k1) to end [30 sts].
Rows 5–15: Beg with a p row, work in stocking stitch (one row purl, one row knit).
Row 16: (k1, sl1, k1, psso) 10 times [20 sts].
Row 18: (sl1, k1, psso) to end [10 sts].
Row 19: (p2tog) 5 times [5 sts].
Cut yarn and thread through rem sts.

Calyx

**With 2.25mm (UK 13; US 1) needles and sage green four-ply yarn, cast on 1 st.
Row 1: inc2 [3 sts].
Row 2: p.
Row 3: k1, (yfwd, k1) twice [5 sts].
Row 4: p.
Row 5: k2, yfwd, k1, yfwd, k2 [7 sts].
Row 6: p.
Row 7: k3, yfwd, k1, yfwd, k3 [9 sts].
Row 8: p.
Row 9: k4, yfwd, k1, yfwd, k4 [11 sts].
Cut yarn and transfer sts to a spare needle **, then rep from ** to ** three times more but do not cut yarn after last repeat.
Row 10: k across all sts [44 sts].
Row 11: p4, (p3tog, p8) 3 times, p3tog, p4 [36 sts].

Row 12: k3, (sl1, k2tog, psso, k6) 3 times, sl1, k2tog, psso, k3 [28 sts]; cut yarn and join in grey-green.
Row 13: p2, (p3tog, p4) 3 times, p3tog, p2 [20 sts].
Row 14: k1, (sl1, k2tog, psso, k2) 3 times, sl1, k1, psso, k2.
Row 15: p to end; cut yarn and thread through rem 12 sts.

Making up

The last row forms the base of the fruit. With the RS (purl side) facing, join the side seam by grafting, then stuff the piece firmly. Run yarn through each stitch of the cast-on edge and pull up to close the opening. Stitch the ends of the leaf section, then run yarn through each of the stitches on the straight edge and pull up. Stitch the leaf section in place on top of the Sharon fruit. The finished Sharon fruit measures approximately 10cm (4in) high and 15cm (6in) in diameter.

Variation

To make a physalis, follow the calyx pattern on this page, using four-ply cotton yarn in grey-green. Make the fruit using orange cotton DK and following the pattern for the cherry on page 24, working rows 1–6, then 5 rows in stocking stitch on 18 stitches, then completing rows 16–19. Place the fruit inside the calyx and secure with a few stitches.

Physalis Attraction

Sharon fruits are variations of persimmon, and they get their name from Israel, where they are grown extensively. Physalis are delicious fruits that, surprisingly, are from the nightshade family.

Fig

Materials:

2 balls DK wool or wool blend yarn – 1 purple, 1 green

Small amount of DK wool or wool blend yarn – pale peach

Polyester fibrefill

Tapestry needle

Needles:

Set of four double-pointed 2.75mm (UK 12; US 2) double-pointed knitting needles

Instructions:

Fig

With four 2.75mm (UK 12; US 2) double-pointed needles and purple yarn, cast on 9 sts and distribute between three needles.

Round 1: k.

Round 2: inc1 in each st [18 sts].

Round 3: (k1, inc1) 9 times [27 sts].

Round 4: (k2, inc1) 9 times [36 sts].

Knit 13 rounds; do not cut yarn but join in green.

Round 18: (k1 green, k1 purple) to end.

Round 19: as round 18.

Cut purple yarn and k2 rounds in green.

Round 22: with green yarn, (k2, sl1, k1, psso) 9 times [27 sts].

Rounds 23–24: k.

Round 25: (k1, sl1, k1, psso) 9 times [18 sts].

Do not cut green yarn but join in pale peach yarn.

Round 26: (k1 green, k1 pale peach) to end.

Round 27: as round 26.

Cut green yarn and cont in pale peach yarn.

Round 28: (sl1, k1, psso) 9 times [9sts].

Round 29: (k1, sl1, k1, psso) 3 times [6 sts].

Rounds 30–33: k.

Round 34: (k2tog tbl) 3 times [3 sts].

Continue on 2 needles only.

Next row: k3, do not turn but slip sts to other end of needle.

Rep last row once more; change to green yarn and rep last row 4 times more. Cast off.

Making up

Add stuffing after completing round 29. Weave in all of the yarn ends. The finished fig measures approximately 8cm (3⅛in) high and 5cm (2in) in diameter.

Variation

For a slightly easier version that avoids having to work two different colours in a row, work in simple stripes instead. Follow the pattern to round 4, then knit 15 rounds; change to green yarn, knit 2 rounds, then work rounds 22–25 before changing to pale peach and then work to the end.

Forever Figs

Figs have an extremely long history in agriculture, and were amongst the earliest cultivated fruits. They are mentioned in the Bible and the Koran, and appear in numerous proverbs, sayings and myths from cultures all over the world.

Blackberry

Materials:

1 ball four-ply wool or wool blend yarn – navy blue

Small amount of DK wool or wool blend yarn – green

Polyester fibrefill

Size 9/0 glass rocaille beads, purple

Tapestry needle

Needles:

1 pair 2.00mm (UK 14; US 0) knitting needles

Two 2.00mm (UK 14; US 0) double-pointed knitting needles

Instructions:

Blackberry

Before starting to knit, thread 90 beads on to yarn.

With 2.00mm (UK 14; US 0) needles and prepared yarn, cast on 10 sts.

Row 1: k each st tbl.

Row 2: k1, inc1 in each st to end [19 sts].

Row 3: *k1, insert needle into next st, push 1 bead to back of st just worked, complete k st, rep from * to last st, k1.

Row 4: p1, insert needle purlwise into next st, push one bead up to front of st just worked, then complete p st; rep from * to end.

Rows 5–12: rep rows 3 and 4.

Row 13: k1, (k2tog) 9 times [10 sts].

Cut yarn and thread through rem sts.

Stalk

With 2.00mm (UK 14; US 0) double-pointed needles and green four-ply yarn, cast on 2 sts.

Row 1: k2; do not turn but slide sts to other end of needle.

Rep row 1 9 times more; cast off.

Making up

Complete the blackberry by stitching the edges (row ends) together to form a tube, then pull up the yarn to gather the top, trapping one end of the stalk. Knot a few short strands of green yarn around the base of the stalk and trim each strand to about 3mm (⅛in). The finished blackberry measures approximately 2.25cm (⅞in) high, excluding the stalk.

Blackberry Surprise

Try varying the colours of the beads and the yarn as you make a punnet's worth. Unripe blackberries are red, so try using all red beads, or half red and half purple. These small variations will make the group look more natural.

Tropical Duo

Materials:

2 balls four-ply cotton yarn – red and creamy yellow

2 balls DK cotton or bamboo blend yarn – pale green and creamy yellow

Small amount of DK or tapestry yarn – yellow ochre

Polyester fibrefill

Tapestry needle

Needles:

Set of four 3.00mm (UK 11; US 2) double-pointed knitting needles

Instructions:

Knitting note:
Yarn is used double throughout.

Mango
With 3.00mm (UK 11; US 2) double-pointed needles and two strands of yarn, cast on 12 sts and distribute between three needles.
Round 1: k.
Round 2: inc1 in each st [24 sts].
Round 3: k.
Round 4: (inc1, k1) 12 times [36 sts].
Rounds 5–7: k.
Round 8: (inc1, k2) 12 times [48 sts].
Rounds 9–19: k to end; cut 1 strand of red yarn and join in 1 strand of yellow yarn.
Rounds 20–21: Knit 2 rounds using red and yellow together. Cut red yarn and continue using two strands of yellow.
Round 22: (k2tog, k2) 12 times [36 sts].
Rounds 23–28: k.
Round 29: (k2tog, k1) 12 times [24 sts].
Rounds 30–37: k.
Round 38: (k2tog, k2) 6 times [18 sts].
Round 39: (k2tog, k1) 6 times [12 sts].
Round 40: (k2tog) 6 times [6 sts].
Round 41: (k2tog) 3 times.
Cut yarn, thread through rem 3 sts; fasten off.

Papaya
With 3.00mm (UK 11; US 2) double-pointed needles and two strands of yarn (one green, one creamy yellow), cast on 12 sts and distribute between three needles.
Round 1: k.
Round 2: inc1 in each st [24 sts].
Round 3: k.
Round 4: (inc1, k1) 12 times [36 sts].
Rounds 5–7: k.
Round 8: (inc1, k2) 12 times [48 sts].
Rounds 9–22: k to end; cut green yarn and continue with two strands of yellow.
Round 23: (k2tog, k2) 12 times [36 sts].
Rounds 24–32: k.
Round 33: (k2tog, k1) 12 times [24 sts].
Rounds 34–37: k to end; cut one strand of yellow yarn, join in one strand of green.
Rounds 38–41: k to end.
Round 42: (k2tog) 12 times; cut yellow yarn and continue to end with 2 strands green.
Rounds 43–44: k.
Round 45: (k2tog) 6 times.
Cut yarn and thread through rem 6 sts; fasten off.

Making up
For both fruits, pull up the tail of yarn on the last row to close up the gap, and fasten off. Insert stuffing through the small hole in the base, then run the strand of yarn through each stitch of cast-on row, pull up to close and fasten off. Flatten the mango slightly. With yellow ochre yarn, embroider a circle of stitches, about 1cm (½in) in diameter, at the stalk end. The finished mango is approximately 10cm (4in) long, while the papaya is 12cm (4¾in) long. Both fruits measure approximately 8cm (3⅛in) in diameter at their widest points.

Papaya and Mango

Originating on opposite sides of the globe, these tempting tropical fruits are equally delicious!

Plum

Materials:

1 ball four-ply wool or wool blend yarn – violet

Small amount of DK yarn – brown

Polyester fibrefill

Tapestry needle

Needles:

1 pair 2.25mm (UK 13; US 1) knitting needles

Two 3.00mm (UK 11; US 2) double-pointed
   knitting needles

Instructions:

Plum

With 2.25mm (UK 13; US 1) needles and violet
four-ply yarn, cast on 6 sts.
Row 1: inc1 in each st to end [12 sts].
Row 2: p.
Row 3: k.
Row 4: p.
Row 5: inc1 in each st to end [24 sts].
Rows 6–8: as rows 2–4.
Row 9: (k1, inc1) 12 times [36 sts].
Rows 10–26: Beg with a p row, work in st st
(1 row purl, 1 row knit).
Row 27: (k1, k2tog) 12 times [24 sts].
Rows 28–30: as rows 2–4.
Row 31: (k2tog) 12 times [12 sts].
Rows 32–34: as rows 2–4.
Row 35: (k2tog) 6 times.
Cut yarn, leaving a tail, and thread through rem
6 sts.

Stalk

With two 3.00mm (UK 11; US 2) double-
pointed needles and brown DK yarn,
cast on 2 sts.
Row 1: k2; do not turn but slide sts to
other end of needle.
Rep row 1 until stalk measures 2cm
(¾in); cast off.

Making up

With the right sides together, stitch the seam
in backstitch, leaving a small opening. Turn the
right sides out, stuff firmly and close the seam,
pulling it up slightly. Next, take the needle
through the plum from the top (cast-on edge)
to the bottom. Pull the yarn gently to create a
dimple in the top, then fasten off. Attach the
stem by threading the yarn end into a needle
and passing the needle down through the
plum from top to bottom. The finished plum
is approximately 6cm (2⅜in) tall (excluding the
stalk) and 5.5cm (2¼in) in diameter.

Plum Crazy
Plums are very versatile, and can be eaten as they are or made into jam, puddings, wine or even brandy – while this knitted version makes a permanent fruity decoration or gift.

Pomegranate

Materials:

1 ball DK wool or wool blend lightweight
   yarn – burgundy

Small amount of DK yarn – yellow ochre

Polyester fibrefill

Stitch holder

Tapestry needle

Needles:

Set of four 2.75mm (UK 12; US 2) double-
   pointed knitting needles

Instructions:

Pomegranate

With set of four 2.75mm (UK 12; US 2) double-
pointed needles and burgundy yarn, cast on 9
sts and distribute between three needles.

Rounds 1 and 2: k.

Round 3: inc1 in each st [18 sts].

Round 4 (and each even-numbered round): k.

Round 5: (k1, inc1) 9 times [27 sts].

Round 7: (k2, inc1) 9 times [36 sts].

Round 9: (k3, inc1) 9 times [45 sts].

Round 11: (k4, inc1) 9 times [54 sts].

Round 13: (k5, inc1) 9 times [63 sts].

Rounds 14–33: k.

Round 34: (k5, k2tog) 9 times [54 sts].

Round 35: (k4, k2tog) 9 times [45 sts].

Round 36: (k3, k2tog) 9 times [36 sts].

Round 37: (k7, k2tog) 4 times [32 sts].

Round 38: (k6, k2tog) 4 times [28 sts].

Round 39: (k5, k2tog) 4 times [24 sts].

Round 40: (k4, k2tog) 4 times [20 sts].

Round 41: k5, turn and leave rem sts on holder;
work on these 5 sts only.

** Row 1: p.

Row 2: k.

Row 3: p.

Row 4: sl1, k1, psso, k1, k2tog.

Row 5: p.

Row 6: sl1, k2tog, psso.

Fasten off.**

Rejoin yarn to sts on holder and rep from ** to
** 3 times more.

Crown

With two needles and yellow ochre yarn, cast
on 10 sts.

Row 1: p.

Row 2: inc1 in each st [20 sts].

Row 3: p.

Row 4: k5, turn and work on these 5 sts only.
Complete four 'points' by following instructions
for pomegranate from ** to **.

Making up

Close up the base of the pomegranate by
threading the yarn through all the stitches on
the cast-on row, then pulling the yarn up tightly
and fastening it off. Insert stuffing through the
hole in the top. Stitch the ends of the crown
together, then place it inside the opening
at the top, where it forms a lining. Slip stitch
each point in place. The finished pomegranate
measures approximately 8cm (3⅛in) tall and
9cm (3½in) in diameter at its widest point.

Tempting Pomegranate

Looking just as beautiful and tempting as a real pomegranate, this one has no annoying seeds!

Apples

Materials:

2 balls DK wool or wool blend yarn – 1 green (A) and 1 red (B)

Small amount of DK yarn – brown

Polyester fibrefill

Tapestry needle

Needles:

1 pair 3.25mm (UK 10; US 3) knitting needles,

Two 3.00mm (UK 11; US 2) double-pointed knitting needles

Instructions:

Large green apple

With 3.25mm (UK 10; US 3) needles and green yarn, cast on 12 sts.
Row 1 (RS): k to end.
Row 2: p to end.
Row 3: inc1 in each st to end [24 sts].
Row 4: p to end.
Row 5: (inc1, k1) 12 times [36 sts].
Row 6: p to end.
Row 7: k1 (inc1, k2) 11 times, inc1, k1 [48 sts].
Rows 8–24: Beg with a p row, work in st st (1 row purl, 1 row knit).
Row 25: k1, k2tog, *k2, k2tog; rep from * to last st, k1 [36 sts].
Row 26: p to end.
Row 27: (k1, k2tog) 12 times [24 sts].
Row 28: (p2tog) 12 times [12 sts].
Row 29: (k2tog) 6 times [6 sts].
Cut yarn, leaving a tail. Thread through rem sts.

Small red and green apple

With two 3.00mm (UK 11; US 2) double-pointed needles and green yarn (A), cast on 12 sts.
Row 1 (RS): k to end.
Row 2: p to end.
Row 3: inc1 in each st to end [24 sts].
Row 4: p to end.
Row 5: (inc1, k1) 12 times [36 sts]. Continue in stocking stitch without further shaping, introducing red yarn (B) as follows:
Row 6: p13A, p12B, p12A.
Row 7: k11A, k14B, k11A.
Row 8: p10A, p16B, p10A.
Row 9: k9A, k18B, k9A.

Row 10: p8A, p20B, p8A.
Row 11: k7A, k22B, k7A.
Row 12: p6A, p24B, p6A.
Row 13: k5A, k26B, k5A.
Row 14: p4A, p28B, p4A.
Row 15: k3A, k30B, k3A.
Row 16: p2A, p32B, p2A. Cut green yarn (A) and continue with red (B).
Row 17: k to end.
Row 18: p to end.
Row 19: k to end.
Row 20: (p1, p2tog) 12 times [24 sts].
Row 21: (k2tog) 12 times [12 sts].
Row 22: (p2tog) 6 times [6 sts].
Cut yarn, leaving a tail. Thread through rem sts.

Stalk

With brown yarn and two 3.25mm double-pointed needles, cast on 3 sts.
Row 1: k3; do not turn but slide sts to other end of needle.
Rep row 1 until cord measures 4cm; cut yarn, leaving a tail, and fasten off.

Making up

Graft the sides (row ends) together to form a neat, invisible seam. Stuff the piece quite firmly with polyester fibrefill, then pull up the tail of the yarn to close the stitches on the last row. Close up the hole in the base in a similar way. Thread the tail of the yarn at the base of the stalk on to a tapestry needle and thread the needle down through the centre of the apple and pull slightly to create an indentation in the top. At the top of the stalk, thread the tail of the yarn in and out of the last two stitches to create a knobbly end. The finished apple measures approximately 6cm (2⅜in) high and 8cm (3⅛in) in diameter.

Scrumping!
Would you Adam 'n' Eve it? This pair of sweet-looking apples should be enough to tempt anyone.

Apple Core

Materials:

2 balls DK wool or wool blend yarn – 1 green, 1 white

Small amount of DK yarn – brown

Polyester fibrefill

Tapestry needle

Needles:

Set of four 3.00mm (UK 11; US 2) double-pointed knitting needles

Instructions:

Apple core

With set of four 3.00mm (UK 11; US 2) double-pointed needles and green yarn, cast on 6 sts and distribute between three needles.
Round 1: inc1 in each st [12 sts].
Round 2: k to end.
Round 3: (k1, inc1) 6 times [18 sts].
Round 4: k to end.
Round 5: (k2, inc1) 6 times [24 sts].
Round 6: k to end; cut yarn and join in white.
Rounds 7–9: With white yarn, k to end.
Round 10: (sl1, k1, psso, k6) 3 times [21 sts].
Rounds 11–13: k to end.
Round 14: (sl1, k1, psso, k5) 3 times [18 sts].
Rounds 15–17: k to end.
Round 18: (sl1, k1, psso, k4) 3 times [15 sts].
Round 19: k to end.
Round 20: (sl1, k1, psso, k3) 3 times [12 sts].
Rounds 21–26: k to end.
Round 27: (inc1, k3) 3 times [15 sts].
Round 28: k to end.
Round 29: (inc1, k4) 3 times [18 sts].
Rounds 30–32: k to end.
Round 33: (inc1, k5) 3 times [21 sts].
Rounds 34–35: k to end.
Round 36: (inc1, k6) 3 times [24 sts].
Rounds 37–38: k, then cut white yarn and join in green.
Round 39: k to end.
Round 40: (k2, k2tog) 6 times [18 sts].
Round 41: k to end.
Round 42: (k1, k2tog) 6 times [12 sts].
Round 43: k to end.

Round 44: (k2tog) 6 times.
Cut yarn and thread through rem 6 sts.

Stalk

With brown yarn and two 3.00mm (UK 11; US 2) double-pointed needles, cast on 2 sts.
Row 1: k2; do not turn but slide sts to other end of needle.
Rep row 1 until cord measures 4cm; cut yarn, leaving a tail, and fasten off.

Making up

Stuff the apple core quite firmly with polyester fibrefill after completing round 37, then continue knitting. Thread the tapestry needle with the tail of the yarn at the base of the stalk, then thread the needle down through the centre of the apple core and pull it slightly to create an indentation in the top. At the top of the stalk, thread the tail of yarn in and out of the last two stitches to create a knobbly end. Use brown yarn to embroider pips in detached chain stitch. The finished apple core is 8cm (3⅛in) tall (excluding the stalk) and 3.5cm (1½in) in diameter.

Finished!
The remains of a delicious snack, a knitted apple core makes a fun gift.

Acknowledgements

A big 'thank you' to Roz Dace for commissioning me to do this book and the others in the series; and to Edd Ralph, editor and project manager.

Thank you to everyone who has supplied me with yarns, including knitshop.co.uk, Sirdar, Rowan and Patons.

Thanks also to members of Knitting Night at The Pelton for their encouragement and feedback.

You are invited to visit the author's website:
www.susieatthecircus.typepad.com

Susie is also a member of the Ravelry online knitting community:
www.ravelry.com

Publishers' Note

If you would like more books about novelty knitting, try:

Knitted Flowers by Susie Johns, Search Press 2009;
Knitted Cakes by Susan Penny, Search Press 2008;
and *Knitted Bears* by Val Pierce, Search Press 2009;
all from the Twenty to Make series.